BIRD WATCH

Designed by Megan R. Youngquist

Edited by Carolyn M. Clark

Developed by C. Douglas Elliott

Foreword by Jay D. Hair

Introduction by Jerome A. Jackson

Photography and captions by Bates Littlehales

ISBN 0-912347-58-9

Printed in Japan by Dai Nippon Printing Co., Ltd.

5 4 3 2 1   97 96 95 94 93 92 91 90

(Pages 2-3) The white-winged dove, a tropical species wintering on the Gulf Coast and in Mexico and Central America, is well adapted to the desert heat. Gregarious, it sometimes nests in sizable colonies, and its cooing "who-cooks-for-you" song is a common sound in any southwestern habitat that provides its preferred seeds, water, and protection.
ZENAIDA ASIATICA

BIRD WATCH

Photography by

BATES LITTLEHALES

Introduction by

JEROME A. JACKSON

Foreword by

JAY D. HAIR

Starwood Publishing, Inc.
Washington, D.C.

*P*erhaps our interest in birds begins with our fascination with flight. Maybe it comes from our love of their natural grace and beauty. Whatever the case, bird watching is more than mere fancy—it's big business in this country. Approximately one-third of the United States population feeds wild birds. The government estimates that each year more than a billion dollars is spent on bird seed and more than $220 million on bird baths, bird houses, and bird feeders!

With the help of binoculars and backyard bird feeders many of us have developed a greater appreciation for nature through simply observing our feathered cohabitants of planet Earth. That appreciation has produced some inspiring examples of conservation.

Jim Johnson of Missouri could tell a few. For 18 years he has helped the U.S. Fish and Wildlife Service track the ruby-throated hummingbird. In fact, at the height of summer Jim and his wife Anne feed 50 to 60 hummingbirds a gallon of sugar water each day.

Art Aylesworth has devoted the past 15 years to helping the mountain bluebird, enticing neighbors and friends throughout the state of Montana to build 18,000 nesting boxes.

Similar work is going on all over this country; such personal commitment is the very essence of the conservation movement. With the dedication of bird lovers like Jim, Anne, Art, and yourself, this planet has real hope for survival.

In *Silent Spring* Rachel Carson wrote, "Over increasingly large areas of the United States, spring now comes unheralded by the return of the birds, and the early mornings are strangely silent where once they were filled with the beauty of bird song." Fortunately, the dark winter of environmental indifference is ending. A new season of action is upon us. And future generations of children, like the replenishing birds, will surely sing its praises.

Jay D. Hair
PRESIDENT,
NATIONAL WILDLIFE FEDERATION

(Facing) The common barn-owl, a nocturnal hunter over open country, preys largely, but not exclusively, on rodents. The feathered discs of its heart-shaped face are believed to help pinpoint and amplify sounds from moving prey, much as TV dishes receive satellite signals. Sounds are heard differently in each of its assymetrical ears, which also aids in locating potenital prey.
TYTO ALBA

*I*t's okay, Mom. It's just that crazy man who watches the birds."

The five-year-old boy, warned by the barking of his dog, had seen me arrive day after day to spend several minutes watching a red-headed woodpecker nest in the utility pole in his front yard. I suppose that my beaten-up Volkswagen, tattered shorts, sweaty T-shirt, Army-surplus jungle hat, and constant peering through binoculars weren't exactly trappings he would have associated with a "normal" person.

Now the mother was at the door, smiling a bit sheepishly, her expression apologizing for her son's comment.

I had noticed the boy before. All of a sudden I realized that I had been blind to his curiosity.

"Come watch this woodpecker chop a grasshopper into pieces for his babies." I beckoned, and the mother pushed the screen door open. He was out in a flash.

"Where is the nest? I don't see a nest. Where are the babies? How do you know there are babies? Why do they eat grasshoppers? I'll bet grasshoppers taste yucky!"

That first day with Jimmy was almost unbearable. The barrage of questions seemed endless. But after a week I was impressed with Jimmy's patience and his perception of what was happening at the nest. When I arrived in the early afternoon, he was already watching, anxious to tell me that both adults had just fed their young and that one of the babies had stuck its head way out of the nest hole.

I'm sure Jimmy will never forget what he learned from those red-headed woodpeckers because he discovered it for himself. And, much more important than identifying the foods the woodpeckers were eating, I learned that by sharing "my" birds with Jimmy, I was able to channel and nurture his curiosity, and that his enthusiasm drew his parents' interest. The day the young fledged, Jimmy's mother called a neighbor over, and I heard her carefully pointing out the plumage differences between adults and juveniles and lecturing on the valuable service the birds provided by feeding on harmful insects. No longer was bird watching a crazy activity.

My own introduction—or at least what I remember as my introduction to the natural world—came when I was nine years old and began delivering the *Des Moines Register* in Middletown, Iowa. Every morning, 365 days a year for 9 years, I was out by 5 a.m. delivering the papers. My world at 5 a.m. in a small midwestern town was the dawn chorus of robins, cardinals, brown thrashers, and a dozen other birds in spring, the feeder frenzy of finches on a cold winter morning, and the diving of purple martins at my dog as we passed their apartment house. Then there was the mystery bird with iridescent feathers, white spots all over, a bright yellow beak, and the ability to mimic a bobwhite. I was enthralled with my first starling!

(Facing) The fall-plumaged palm warbler at its least colorful stage contrasts with the bayberry at its most. Migrating from nesting grounds in northern sphagnum bogs, the palm warbler will eat bayberries such as these on the Virginia coast, but it is more likely to be seen farther south, working the ground for insects. Grassy areas along the Anhinga Trail in Florida's Everglades National Park are good places to study this bird from winter to early spring.
DENDROICA PALMARUM

I wouldn't trade those hours for anything; each morning meant new discoveries, new adventures: seven migrant sandhill cranes honking overhead, a house wren's nest in a clothesline pole, a pied-billed grebe turned kamikaze by mistakenly diving into a wet asphalt parking lot that must have looked like a placid pond in the twilight. One Thanksgiving morning I returned from my route to find three wild turkeys perched in the catalpa tree in my front yard.

How could I ignore birds—their sounds, their color, their behavior, their diversity? The inquisitiveness inspired and nurtured by birds became my passport to the whole living world. Ears listening for birds soon heard frogs, toads, and insects; eyes looking for birds and their nests became aware of flowers and patterns of bark, branches, and leaves that differed from one kind of tree or bush to another, yet were wonderfully repetitive among the same kind.

House sparrows jumping, flying, hopping, zigging, zagging, hovering in the light from a grocery store in the predawn introduced me to the micromonsters—the wonderful world of click beetles, stag beetles, buffalo treehoppers, lacewings, and other insects that I visualized as shrunken beasts from the time of the dinosaurs. Each morning a new array of them clung to screens and walls, their tiny horns, bulging eyes, fierce mandibles, and bizarre patterns earning them a short stay in my mayonnaise jar zoo.

I became an intense student of animal behavior. As I made "revolutionary" discoveries, I began keeping a journal of my observations. Red-winged blackbird nests in cattails were so much bigger than those in bushes. A killdeer vigorously shook its foot in a puddle before grabbing a worm. Chimney swifts often flew in squadrons of three.

I doubt now that my childhood discoveries of the natural world were unique. Some of my notes were downright silly—but I was hooked. The living world was important to me, and in some miniscule way I knew that I was important to it. Such recognition of an interdependence between humans and the world around them is to conservation a germinating seed. It is a recognition that comes to us as individuals and must be acted upon by us as individuals.

The conservation movement as we know it today was born in the late 1800s in response to the decimation of herons, egrets, terns, and other birds for the use of their feathers as ornamentation on women's clothes. At first a few voices were heard decrying the slaughter, but in the end thousands of individuals refused to wear feathers and urged the passage of bird protection laws. The movement spawned the National Audubon Society, the American Ornithologists' Union, and other organizations, and led to the enactment of federal and state laws and international treaties which protected birds. This was a popular movement, involving the average individual as well as the concerned scientist. Once the recognition of value in the natural world was sparked, the movement grew and metamorphosed as the audience wanted to know more about birds.

The use of feathers on women's clothes was not the only activity that was hurting bird populations in the late 1800s. At that time the collection of birds' eggs and skins was as popular as stamp, coin, or baseball card collecting in more recent years. The then-fledgling Sears Roebuck Company sold special cabinets for collectors to display their eggs.

When the collection of birds and their eggs was outlawed, interest in birds didn't die.

It was redirected. Bird watching, today simply called birding, was born. The trophy brought home from a day afield was the tally of species seen. Competitive birding—the lure of the list—fostered growth of local clubs. Individuals such as Ludlow Griscom demonstrated that birds could be quickly identified in the field by learning a few distinctive plumage and behavioral characteristics. One of Ludlow's friends, Roger Tory Peterson, added impetus to birding as a sport by the publication of *A Field Guide to the Birds of Eastern North America.* Technological advances spawned by the military needs of two world wars also contributed to the growth of birding. Binoculars, spotting scopes, and photographic equipment became more refined and readily available.

The technological boom associated with World War II also provided us with DDT and other organochlorine pesticides that promised to save us from the scourge of insect pests. Fortunately we were watching the birds. The deaths of American robins on the Michigan State University campus after DDT spraying and thin-shelled eggs of ospreys, brown pelicans, and other birds alerted us to the dangers of these chemicals. The ecology movement of the 1960s involved concern for the whole living world, but scrutiny of this movement would reveal a foundation based on the watching of birds. Birds provided a bridge to the natural world that joined both scientists and amateurs.

Why do birds play such a pivotal role in our relationship with the living world? Often I ask my students what event, what plant or animal drew their attention to nature. Most frequently the reply involves birds. Birds are conspicuous, found in virtually every environment that man frequents. Aside from their ubiquity and willingness to accept our offerings of food, water, and nesting sites, our interactions with birds have been greatly influenced by four characteristics which humans and most birds have in common: both are active during the day, both have color vision, both have extensive vocal repertoires, and both have complex social interactions including parental care.

The first two of these shared characteristics are related. The cells in bird and human eyes that allow color vision don't function in dim light or at night. Most mammals, and birds such as nightjars and owls, that are active at night have eyes specialized for detecting form and movement in minimal light, but lack the cells sensitive to color. We find color vision is a characteristic of animals active during the day. Birds and humans, with their ability to see color, can use it to communicate. The functions of color in the lives of birds and humans have been honed to perfection through time and innumerable generations. Color is important in recognition of species and individuals. It is important in courtship and territorial defense. The amount, position, and display of red on a woodpecker may indicate that he is looking for a mate. When accompanied by the appropriate human behavior, the polished red sports car of a human male may send a similar message.

The songs, calls, and mechanical sounds produced by birds are often the first evidence we detect of their presence. Their language is unlike ours—more melodious by our standards—and is produced by different structures. Yet the predictability of each species' song allows us to readily identify the singer, and in a sense knowing identity bestows ownership.

Finding a nest and watching the parents care for their eggs and young is one of the

(Pages 12-13) At Bosque del Apache NWR, New Mexico, massed snow geese join sandhill cranes in harvesting the abundant grain planted specifically for wildlife and the insects attracted to it. Difficult, but not impossible, is picking out among the crowd a smaller look-alike of the snow goose, the rare Ross' goose.
CHEN CAERULESCENS

simple things in life that fascinates and cheers people of all ages. It's easy to think that the human parents of the world should emulate the birds' dedicated actions, but their actions are not so much ones of reason (as we like to think of ours) as they are of instinct. A bird's response to nest and eggs are entirely predetermined.

A few years ago my wife and I had a number of killdeer nests under observation. One morning we went to visit a nest at which the clutch of four eggs had just been completed and the parents had more than 20 days of incubation ahead of them to hatch the eggs. When we arrived, we found that a lawn mower had destroyed the eggs. Three hours later we saw a nest where one of the adults had been killed by a predator and the other parent was missing, yet an egg had hatched that morning and three more were pipped and would hatch within a day. We waited an hour to see if the missing parent would return, but it didn't. Knowing that the chicks could not survive on their own, we took the chick and eggs to the nest site destroyed by the mower. Within ten minutes the chick and eggs were adopted, and the foster parents behaved as always when chicks are hatching, never once noticing that the 20-day incubation period sped by in a few hours.

Even if we didn't share noticeable traits, man's aspirations of flight alone would have garnered a special place for birds in the mythology and history of most, if not all, human cultures. The power of flight led to the belief that birds could be messengers to or from the gods. The Athenians of ancient Greece would see little owls nesting atop the pillars of their temple, and the owl became associated with their goddess. When the Greeks were about to be attacked by a Persian force much larger than their own, they were rallied by the sight of an owl flitting in the moonlight—a sign from their goddess— and the Persians were routed.

For Christopher Columbus and his crews, the flight of land birds near their ships in the autumn of 1492 was not merely an omen, but a signpost indicating that land was near and giving the explorers inspiration to forge ahead.

Just as the owl was the gatekeeper at the Temple of Athena and birds the greeters at the fringe of our continent, so too they have served us as omens and messengers leading the way in the scientific understanding of animal behavior. Keeping an eye on birds has often brought us face to face with discoveries about our own nature. The following are but a few examples.

Mockingbirds of the Galapagos Islands were central figures in Charles Darwin's discovery of the principle of natural selection and development of the concept of evolution. Darwin found that populations of mockingbirds on different islands in the archipelago differed slightly from one another as a result of their isolation and adaptation to local conditions.

The defense of food and nest by birds led Elliot Howard to an understanding of territoriality: how and why birds and other animals defend an area as their own, keeping individuals of the same species and same sex at a distance.

G. K. Noble taught us the importance of the physical characteristics by which we and other species identify members of the opposite sex and use this information to distinguish between potential mates and potential competitors for a mate or nest site. His

A great egret at Mattamuskeet NWR, North Carolina, "walks slowly" and "probes"—two terms describing its feeding behavior. In times past the species' considerable beauty nearly led to its demise. A century ago gunners slaughtered egrets for their graceful nuptial plumes called aigrettes, used to adorn women's hats.
CASMERODIUS ALBUS

(Pages 16-17) Atlantic puffins, after feeding their chicks, are ready to return to sea for more fish. Like other pelagic birds, puffins live on the open seas and come ashore only to breed. Machias Seal Island off the coast of Maine supports a viable puffin population near the southernmost part of their breeding range. Introduced rats, dogs, and cats have eradicated colonies from other northern islands.
FRATERCULA ARCTICA

studies involving painting on or obscuring the "moustache" of flickers and noting the response of other birds are considered classic.

Konrad Lorenz pioneered the modern concept of instinctive behavior with his studies of imprinting. He wondered why young goslings would follow their parent soon after hatching, and was able to demonstrate that goslings would follow him as if he were their parent if he crouched down (so that he was no taller than a goose) and was the first moving thing the new hatchlings saw.

Margaret Morse Nice studied song sparrows near her home, using detailed behavioral observation of marked populations of birds to further elaborate on studies of instinct, territoriality, and parental care.

These studies of bird behavior have led to deeper understanding of our own actions. In addition, studies of the relationships of birds to their environments have given us insight into our relationship with the rest of the world.

While similarities in the lives of birds and humans may be a major underlying reason for our fascination with them, one very important difference between us both invites our interest and is leading to the extinction of some birds and the jeopardy of others. Birds are intimately adapted to the environments they frequent. In the camouflaged colors and patterns of the grassland sparrows which match the dried grasses of the prairies, in the perfectly engineered long necks, beaks, and legs of waders who frequent the marshes, each species "fits" in its particular habitat. Man, in contrast, invades all habitats, not by a diversity of physical adaptations but by his ability to alter habitats to suit his needs.

One of the most basic concepts in ecology today is that of the niche, sometimes defined as the role of the organism in its environment. Ornithologist Joseph Grinnell introduced the idea, and other ornithologists have demonstrated that each species living in a community occupies a slightly different niche. This prevents excessive competition among community members. For example, red-bellied woodpeckers keep to wooded areas, whereas red-headed woodpeckers prefer open environments. The more species living in a community, the more narrow and specialized those niches must be.

In recent years biodiversity, the collection of all forms of life in an ecosystem, has become one of the "buzz topics" of educated society. Scientists understand that maintaining species diversity is critical to the stability of ecosystems. They also know that diversity in virtually all major groups of plants and animals increases from the poles to the tropics. The pattern is nowhere better seen than in bird populations, with only a few species occurring in the Arctic, increasing to nearly 400 in the state of Mississippi, and exploding to more than 1,700 species near the equator in Colombia. One effect of such tremendous biodiversity in the tropics is the extreme specialization found among community members. Specialization makes a species more prone to extinction because it is less able to adapt to different food resources and altered habitats. Thus the diversity of tropical ecosystems is particularly vulnerable to change.

The pressures on humans to produce more food and to maximize economic return from every parcel of land have led to destruction of natural habitats and reduction in species diversity. Habitat destruction has become the single greatest cause of species extinction. The concomitant establishment of monocultures of crops and marketable tree species has favored the insect predators on those plants, while eliminating the nesting sites, alternative food resources, and other habitat needs of their natural avian controls. To understand these problems we must realize that not only are birds physically adapted to their particular environments, but they are behaviorally adapted as well. They are genetically programmed to select the "right" habitats.

The concept of niche as further defined by ornithologist Frances James helps us to better understand the unique interrelationships between each bird species and its habitat. In northwestern Arkansas, James searched for nests of many species of birds and recorded the characteristics of each nest site. Within species she began to find certain habitat components that were typically present, often in a specific configuration. From these patterns she concluded that each species has an innate mental picture of an appropriate nest site. James refers to this innate mental picture as the species' "niche gestalt."

The first artist to truly bring us a glimpse of the bird in its own world was John James Audubon. The bird was the focus, but the plants, their flowers and fruits, insects, lizards, snakes, and other creatures were no less realistic. To the extent that these paintings illustrate the species' habitat, they may provide us with some evidence of each species' niche gestalt. Unlike the work of his predecessors, Audubon's paintings often portray the bird in action, as if undisturbed by the artist. Audubon claimed, as did some of his predecessors and many of his followers, to have painted his birds from life, but he did not, nor do the vast majority of artists. Audubon did not have quality binoculars and long-range lenses to study his subjects. He shot them, pinned them to a grid of wire so that he might get precise proportions, and painted them "shortly after" life. As a result, Audubon could not know the bird's expression, the vibrant eye, the subtlety of posture, the anticipation of action. He had to guess what those might be, and in the end he often instilled his birds with the expressions and emotions of humans.

Perhaps such human characteristics have assured the enduring popularity of Audubon's work. The casual observer identifies with the bird. The careful observer may find fault with it.

The camera, in contrast, captures the moment, freezes it, and shows us the true bird. Some may quibble that photographs do not make good field guide illustrations because of variability in light conditions, orientation, and plumage from one bird to the next. Artistic license does allow a painter to portray a bird in archetypal plumage that facilitates human recognition of color and pattern. But a photo of a bird in its natural environment says more. It shows the combination of factors that an experienced birder senses but perhaps can't define. It shows the features of the bird, those of its habitat, and how the two interact. In a sense it defines the interdependence of bird and environment. Every successful photo is an essay, telling innumerable details of the bird's existence and enriching our own. Photographs—each a passport to the bird's world—can be powerful tools in the development of personal involvement with the world around us.

Jerry Jackson

(Pages 20-21) A male house finch, a common bird of the west, perches on a huisache branch in the Arizona desert. Nonexistent in the eastern United States before 1940, house finches were illegally captured in California and sold in the eastern pet trade as "Hollywood finches." To avoid arrest when confronted, dealers released captives to the wild.
CARPODACUS MEXICANUS

(Above and facing) The adaptable house finch fares well in its new eastern home. Its population has grown tremendously and now spreads from New England to the Gulf Coast and Midwest. The bather is a Virginia suburbanite; his ancestors were Californians.

CARPODACUS MEXICANUS

(Facing) A female northern
cardinal bathes to clean
her plumage and stimulate
the oiling and preening
process. Sunbathing *(above)*
prompts this male cardinal
to preen. Some studies have
shown that warmth drives
parasites to accessible spots
for removal; others main-
tain that skin-absorbed
vitamin D from the sun's
rays may prevent rickets.
CARDINALIS CARDINALIS

$\mathcal{B}$y the time the yellow-rumped warbler *(facing)* reaches wintering grounds in the southern United States, he has molted out of breeding plumage into a plainer winter coat which he will again molt before instinctive mating and migrational urges drive him north. His gradual feather loss and replacement does not impair flight.

DENDROICA CORONATA

During spring migration through Virginia this yellow-rumped warbler shows his new breeding plumage which will help attract a mate on northern nesting grounds.

DENDROICA CORONATA

This chestnut-sided warbler shows
none of the color that gives him his
common name. Both sexes molt into
drabber plumage for winter in Central
America. When colorful feathers
are not needed to attract a mate, in-
conspicuousness has its advantages
against predators.
DENDROICA PENSYLVANICA

The male blackburnian warbler acquires a brilliant orange color only as he migrates north to breed. He sings from the very tops of spruce, fir, and larch trees, where his dazzling color catches the female eye and warns off other males.
DENDROICA FUSCA

In fall the scarlet tanager of the eastern woodlands often puzzles the beginning birder, who needs reassurance that this bird can really be bright red with black wings and tail in another season. The tanager is drinking by "head tilt" rather than sucking water like a dove.
PIRANGA OLIVACEA

(Pages 32-33) A remote-controlled camera records the red, open mouths of Savannah sparrows signaling for food. Since the young birds cannot yet see, the gaping behavior is triggered by the sound or movement of the approaching parent. In turn the open beak with its bright color elicits the parent's feeding response.
PASSERCULUS SANDWICHENSIS

On the North Dakota plains
a grasshopper sparrow
proclaims that other males
are not welcome in his
one- to three-acre territory.
Song, like plumage and
body language, attracts a
prospective mate. Not only
do songs vary among
species, they also vary
regionally and even be-
tween individuals of the
same species.

AMMODRAMUS SAVANNARUM

(Facing) A white-crowned
sparrow perches in Cali-
fornia's San Luis NWR.
Although this refuge is
managed primarily for
wintering waterfowl, many
songbirds benefit from the
plentiful seeds in fields
and edges of woods. In
such lush wintering grounds
flocks of up to 50 sparrows
will forage together.

ZONOTRICHIA LEUCOPHRYS

A Savannah sparrow, named for the city in Georgia where Alexander Wilson discovered it in 1811, perches in a grassland in northern California. This sparrow is widely distributed in grasslands and marshes throughout the United States.
PASSERCULUS SANDWICHENSIS

(Pages 38-39) Common in the west and midwest, rare in the east, lark sparrows congregate in small flocks even in the nesting season. Their song, sometimes delivered in the air, is considered by human listeners as one of the most musical among sparrows.
CHONDESTES GRAMMACUS

Until John James Audubon journeyed west on the Missouri River, the western meadowlark was presumed the same species as the eastern. Audubon noted that the song was different and that feather markings, not easily seen unless the specimen was in hand, varied significantly between the species. Audubon named his discovery *Sturnella neglecta*—neglected by other ornithologists.

STURNELLA NEGLECTA

The eastern meadowlark became distinct from its western look-alike many thousands of years ago, when a change in geography separated populations. They gradually—very gradually, according to most experts—differed in ways that could never again be reconciled. Where now the two species' ranges overlap, differences in song and other less obvious signals keep the two from interbreeding.

STURNELLA MAGNA

(Pages 44-45) At home in a wet, sedgy meadow in North Dakota the sedge wren, formerly known as the short-billed marsh wren, is uncommon, local, and shy compared with its cousin the marsh wren who lives among cattails and bulrushes.

CISTOTHORUS PLATENSIS

(Facing) Cedar waxwings are gregarious birds out of the nesting season, flocking together and wandering erratically to gorge on a large variety of berries, including cedar. In towns they consume European mountain ash, pyracantha, privet, and mulberries. Reports of intoxication indicate that the berries are sometimes overripe and fermenting when the birds feed.
BOMBYCILLA CEDRORUM

*A*cedar waxwing sleeps away a cold New Year's Eve, roosting in a Virginia backyard. Unlike most birds who sleep with heads turned and bills tucked into back feathers, the waxwing faces front.
BOMBYCILLA CEDRORUM

(Pages 48-49) Above feeding sandhill cranes in Bosque del Apache NWR, New Mexico, swarms a winter flock of mixed blackbirds—red-winged, yellow-headed, and other species. Flying closely together with amazing synchronization, flocks such as this offer many pairs of eyes to search out food sources and protection from predators who must single out an individual victim.

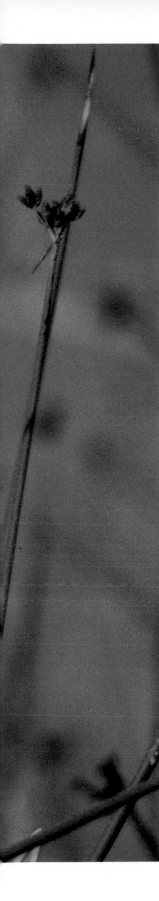

(Facing) A male yellow-headed blackbird sings a croaky courtship song and postures, showing off his plumage in a Utah marsh. Offstage, hopefully, a female is suitably impressed enough to mate.
XANTHOCEPHALUS XANTHOCEPHALUS

In Florida wetlands a red-winged blackbird sets up territory. When the females first arrive, the male puts on a flamboyant show called songspread, singing and holding his wings to exhibit his red epaulets. The last part of the song identifies him to other red-wings. The first part, with its subtle variations, is what gets the girls.
AGELAIUS PHOENICEUS

A Swainson's thrush satisfies its thirst at a Piedmont pool in Virginia. After nesting in northern conifers, it migrates south by night, as do many other species of songbirds. In the morning thirst and the sound of dripping water lure it to pools such as this.
CATHARUS USTULATUS

(Facing) In the Sonoran Desert of Arizona a curve-billed thrasher, its bill adapted for digging vigorously in the ground, perches on an ocotillo branch. This cousin of the mockingbird can readily be seen near water sources in the southwest.
TOXOSTOMA CURVIROSTRE

The Florida subspecies of the scrub jay resides in the flat scrub country on both the east and Gulf coasts. It is becoming rarer as more of its habitat undergoes development.
APHELOCOMA COERULESCENS

(Facing) The Clark's nut-cracker, named for William Clark of the Lewis and Clark expedition, is a member of the crow family. It can become quite tame. Without handouts the Clark's nutcracker does very well on its own, recovering 70% of the seeds it stores for winter, according to one study.
NUCIFRAGA COLUMBIANA

The Carolina chickadee is one of the southeast's favorite freeloaders at backyard feeding stations. Sunflower seeds almost guarantee the chickadee's presence in a suburban yard. Farther north and west the black-capped chickadee predominates.
PARUS CAROLINENSIS

A Carolina chickadee flies off with a sunflower seed. Within their winter territory chickadees forage with titmice, nuthatches, and downy woodpeckers, each species using different feeding strategies to reduce competition.
PARUS CAROLINENSIS

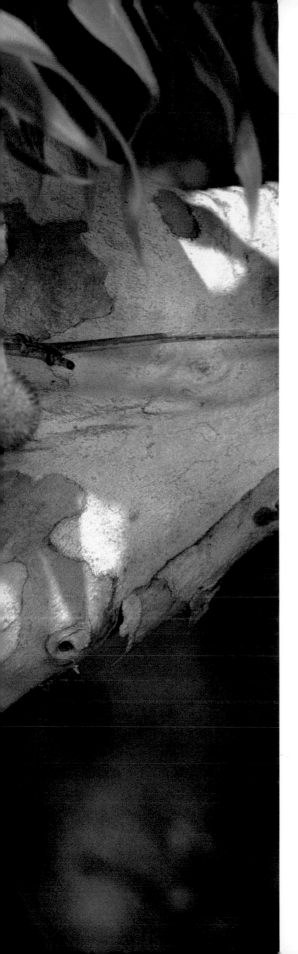

The vermilion flycatcher,
especially fond of bees,
waits for a flying insect to
pass. He will then dart out
and snap it up on the wing.
PYROCEPHALUS RUBINUS

(Facing) A male vermilion
flycatcher attends the nest
in a southeast Arizona
sycamore. The female in-
cubates the eggs, but after
the young hatch, both
parents share nest duties:
brooding the young, shading
them from heat, and re-
moving sacs of fecal waste.
PYROCEPHALUS RUBINUS

The pauraque resides only as far north as south Texas. At Santa Ana NWR bordering the Rio Grande, it is quite common. Many nocturnal animals such as this pauraque have a special layer on the retina, called the *tapetum lucidum*, which gathers any available light to enhance the animal's night vision. It is the *tapetum lucidum* that reflects the light of a camera flash or car headlight and causes the eyes to shine.

NYCTIDROMUS ALBICOLLIS

The Costa's hummingbird builds a nest
of plant material and lichen and binds it
with spider web. The nest of each species
of hummingbird is as distinctive as a
fingerprint. The female, surprisingly
tolerant of a close approach, could not be
positively distinguished from the black-
chinned hummingbird without seeing
this nest in an Arizona desert wash,
although the males are easily recognized.
CALYPTE COSTAE

The ruby-throated hummingbird, the common hummer of eastern North America, flashes red iridescence on its gorget only when light strikes at the correct angle. Its concave feathers are made of cylindrical barbules that act like flat mirrors, reflecting light only in a single direction. The viewer sees red from one angle, and, with a slight change of position, black.

ARCHILOCHUS COLUBRIS

Close cousins in the genus *Melanerpes* are the gila woodpecker *(left)* and the red-bellied woodpecker *(right)*. The gila is a bird of the southwest cactus country, often excavating its nest hole in the giant saguaro. The red-belly is an eastern species ranging to east Texas. This Florida red-belly has chiseled a nesting hole in a sabal palm.

MELANERPES UROPYGIALIS
MELANERPES CAROLINUS

The great horned owl is a powerful predator, flying soundlessly at night and striking its prey with formidable feet and talons. Silent flight is made possible by specialized, sound-dampening barbs on the leading edge of the outermost primary, or flight feather, of its wings.

BUBO VIRGINIANUS

The blue grouse of the western mountains displays during courtship. He inflates air sacs—extensions of his esophagus—on his neck to produce a groaning sound attractive to females. Coloration of the air sacs differs from reddish purple for birds of the Rockies to yellow in coastal mountain areas.

DENDRAGAPUS OBSCURUS

On a courting spot called a lek, or
booming ground, the greater prairie-
chicken struts and inflates his air sacs.
Several cocks compete for a hen's attention; she then mates with the dominant
male. The Texas subspecies called
Attwater's prairie-chicken, shown here,
is listed as endangered. An eastern
subspecies known as the heath hen
has been extinct since 1932.

TYMPANUCHUS CUPIDO

(Facing) The Gambel's quail sports a forward-leaning topknot; the richly colored male wears the same plumage all year. This desert quail's distinctive call notes appear as background in the sound-track of many western movies—even when not appropriate to the habitat.
CALLIPEPLA GAMBELII

In breeding season the willow ptarmigan, a resident of the far north, displays his eye combs. In winter both sexes molt into a completely white plumage to blend with snow. They also grow feathered "snow-shoes" for walking on the powdery surface.
LAGOPUS LAGOPUS

A male willow ptarmigan struts near Hudson Bay in full summer plumage. The hen's feathers blend with the predominantly brownish background of willows, making her difficult for a predator to detect on her nest.
LAGOPUS LAGOPUS

An osprey pair return to their northern Florida territory where they will add to and patch up their old nest before laying eggs. Agricultural use of the pesticide DDT tremendously damaged this fish-eating species that is high on the food chain, but recovery has been steady since the DDT ban.
PANDION HALIAETUS

The adult red-tailed hawk's heavy brow shades the keen eye with which this raptor makes its living. Soaring 100 feet overhead, it can easily spot the mouse that is to be its meal. The red-tail is North America's most widespread hawk, although its numbers have declined in the last 30 years due to persecution and habitat destruction by man.
BUTEO JAMAICENSIS

(Facing) In New Mexico, this immature red-tailed hawk perches in ideal habitat: open country with a woodland border and plenty of rodents, snakes, birds, and even grasshoppers to feed upon. When the red-tail roosts, the great horned owl hunts the same feeding grounds, using hearing to locate prey as efficiently as the red-tail uses vision.
BUTEO JAMAICENSIS

(Facing) An Atlantic puffin spreads its wings on Machias Seal Island. To feed the young chicks snug in rock crevices, the adult flies underwater (instead of swimming with its feet like a duck), turning its head from side to side, picking fish out of a school. The result *(above)* is a beak filled to capacity with capelins facing alternating directions.
FRATERCULA ARCTICA

(Pages 82-83) On both the north Atlantic and Pacific coasts nesting colonies of common murres are supported by vast quantities of coldwater seafood. Members of the *Alcid* family, murres, puffins, and auks occupy an ecological niche very similar to that of penguins in the southern hemisphere.
URIA AALGE

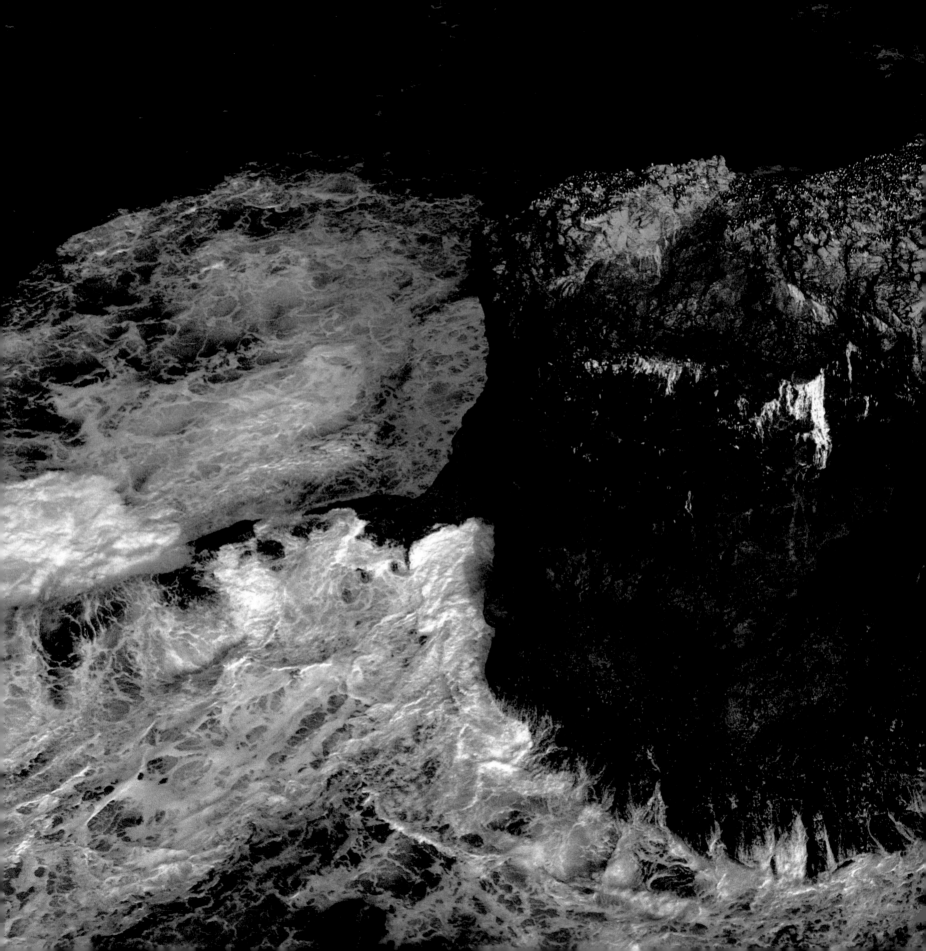

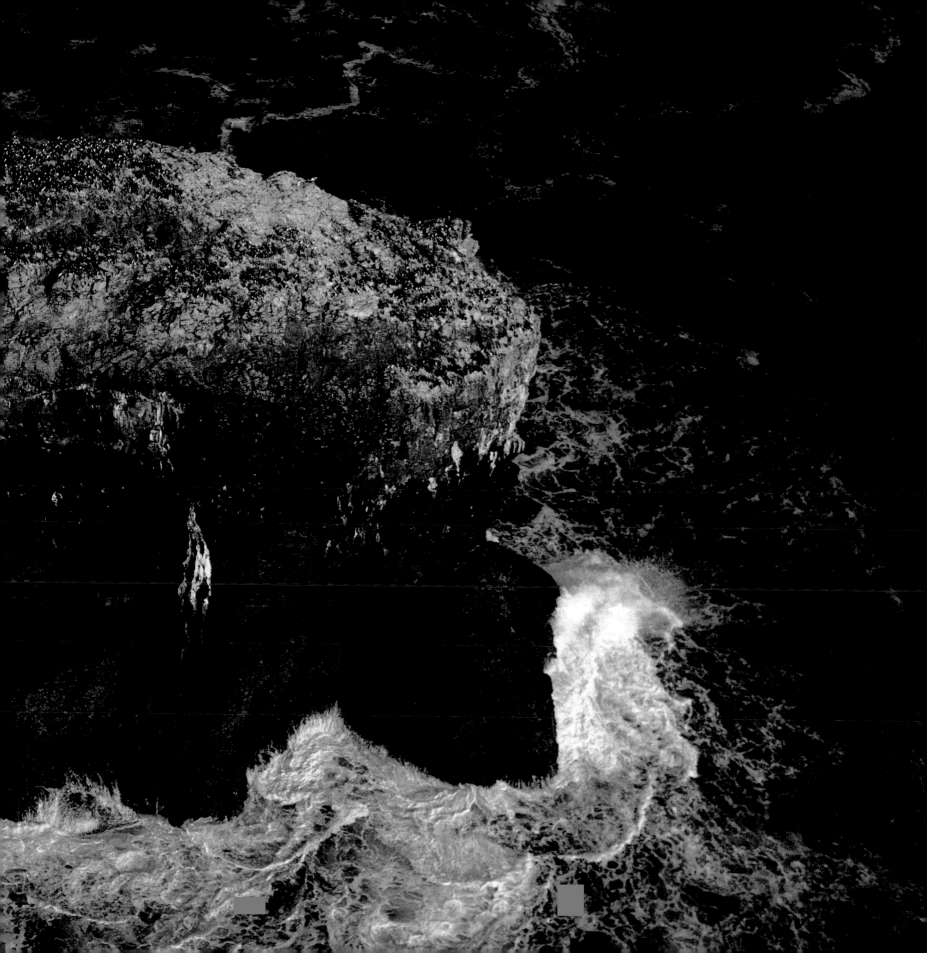

*R*uddy turnstones stage in sizable flocks in Manitoba before migrating farther north to nest on Arctic tundra. While wintering on the southern Atlantic, southern California, and Gulf coasts, turnstones can be seen feeding singly or among other species of shorebirds.

ARENARIA INTERPRES

The American avocet's recurved bill allows
it to feed differently from other shorebirds:
sweeping the bill underwater from side to side
along the bottom and stirring up food, or
skimming midge and mosquito larvae from
just below the surface. The avocet is a social
bird, feeding in groups *(above)*. The bird
rising from the water *(facing)* sounds its
call notes.

RECURVIROSTRA AMERICANA

Long-billed dowitchers
sleep and preen at Klamath
NWR, Oregon, an important
stop between far northern
nesting grounds and the
dowitcher's wintering
grounds from central
California to Guatemala. In
the field long- and short-
billed dowitchers are readily
identified by differences in
their calls: one note for
the long-billed, a three-
note whistle for the
short-billed.
LIMNODROMUS GRISEUS

Not only is the female Wilson's phalarope much richer in color than the male, she may also have more than one mate, laying a clutch for each of her males to incubate. This is one of the few examples of polyandry in the bird world. When she initiates courtship by posturing to the male *(facing)*, he is triggered into the "pounce" *(right)*, which positions him for mating.

PHALAROPUS TRICOLOR

A California gull incubates an egg in a Utah nesting colony. These gulls earned the status of state bird by devouring a swarm of long-horned grasshoppers, thus saving Utah's first Mormon settlers from starvation. Consuming large quantities of crickets, cutworms, and mice also makes the California gull a boon to agriculture.
LARUS CALIFORNICUS

(Facing) A nest of the western gull, with egg and newly hatched chick, sits momentarily unattended in a colony at Farallon Island NWR, California. The chicks are beautifully disguised to blend with their rocky habitat.
LARUS OCCIDENTALIS

A snow goose incubates her eggs near
Hudson Bay. Her color form, the blue morph,
is common among lesser snow geese and
uncommon among the other subspecies,
greater snow geese. This goose will most likely
migrate down the Mississippi flyway to winter
in the Gulf Coast area.
CHEN CAERULESCENS

Goslings snuggle together
in a downy Canada goose
nest on an island in the
Columbia River. Canada
geese are among the
earliest waterfowl to hatch
in the springtime.
BRANTA CANADENSIS

(Pages 96-97) In October
on the Eastern Shore of
Maryland, Canada geese
mass. The geese, which
mate for life, also fly and
forage together in family
groups. Many populations
of Canada geese no
longer migrate.
BRANTA CANADENSIS

At Mattamuskeet NWR, North Carolina, tundra swans
winter in their southernmost large concentration. This
swan is found throughout much of the northern
hemisphere. Until recently, however, the North American
and European populations were regarded as separate
species—the whistling swan and Bewick's swan. To feed,
the tundra swan roots at underwater plants, stimulating
plant growth for subsequent years.
CYGNUS COLUMBIANUS

$\mathcal{I}$n early May a northern shoveler loafs by a Texas lagoon before the migration north. Comblike plates in a large, spatulate beak, almost a caricature of a duck's bill, allow it to strain food from a soupy marsh much as a baleen whale feeds.

ANAS CLYPEATA

(Facing) As long as ice-free, open water is available for feeding, the mallard will not move farther south than its Maryland wintering grounds. Large, game-farm mallards have been widely introduced, and it is believed that these "super" ducks have a competitive advantage partially responsible for declines in black duck populations.

ANAS PLATYRYNCHOS

A hen mallard and her ducklings strike "freeze" postures in a Montana wetland. Camouflaged coloration and a lack of movement often make them invisible to predators. The hen separates from the drake in the nesting season, and, surprisingly, only the hen makes the familiar quacking sound associated with ducks.
ANAS PLATYRYNCHOS

(Pages 104-105) At Red Rocks Lake NWR, Montana, a pair of trumpeter swans shepherd their cygnets along the marsh. When the species was gravely endangered in the lower 48 states, an all-out conservation and management program originating from this refuge raised populations out of the danger zone.
CYGNUS BUCCINATOR

Woods destruction, wetlands (especially swamp) drainage, and overhunting threatened the wood duck population in the early 1900s. Beginning in 1918, the United States and Canada closed hunting for 23 years. Now, with habitat protection and nesting boxes to supplement dead trees needed by these hole-nesting ducks, their population is again viable.
AIX SPONSA

*T*his immature red-breasted merganser winters at Ding Darling NWR, Florida. Unlike most ducks, who feed on vegetation, mergansers are fish eaters, with long, serrated beaks adapted to catching and holding their prey.
MERGUS SERRATOR

(Pages 108-109) Northern pintails resting here at Klamath NWR, Oregon, during fall migration find the food, water, and shelter they need to sustain life. All along the migrational route weather, habitat destruction, and abnormal seasonal conditions affect bird populations, often in a species selective manner.
ANAS ACUTA

An immature black-crowned night-heron plays with a stick at Chincoteague NWR, Virginia. Play, as with all species, prepares the young for work to come: bill manipulation for feeding and also for nest building with sticks like this.
NYCTICORAX NYCTICORAX

(Facing) A green-backed heron in Everglades National Park is rewarded for fishing patiently with almost more than he can manage. The bird remains motionless for long periods of time, leaning from a perch over the water and watching relentlessly. Green-backed herons are also known to use lures in their fishing efforts, dropping a feather, leaf, or piece of debris in the water and waiting to capture the curious fish that comes to investigate.
BUTORIDES STRIATUS

(Facing) The little blue heron nests in isolated forest patches on the edges of wetlands. In its immature stage the little blue heron is white. The great blue heron *(above)* has impaled a mullet on the east coast of Texas.

EGRETTA CAERULEA

ARDEA HERODIAS

A tricolored heron perches in a mangrove on the Florida Gulf Coast. This heron prefers coastal marshes and shores and can be seen feeding on mud flats and in tidal creeks.
EGRETTA TRICOLOR

(Pages 116-117) Against a background of red mangrove roots, a roseate spoonbill loafs near the rest of its flock in Ding Darling NWR. Its flatten- ed, spoon-shaped bill has extreme tactile sensitivity to prey detected by swing- ing it from side to side in mud. Roseate spoonbill populations seem to be growing; sitings have been reported in southern states where the species had never been seen before.
AJAIA AJAJA

(Facing) A flock of white ibis loafs in a Florida marsh. These graceful wading birds forage in flocks and form large communal roosts and nesting colonies. In breeding season their skin parts, legs, and beaks redden noticeably *(above)*.
EUDOCIMUS ALBUS

119

American white pelicans fish in tight, cooperative groups, forming a horseshoe shape to herd schooling fish which they scoop up in their large bill pouches. A grooming brown pelican *(facing)* uses a different feeding strategy: it plunges into the water bill first and pouch-nets the fish while submerged.

PELECANUS OCCIDENTALIS

PELECANUS ERYTHRORYNCHOS

merican white pelicans in a Montana nesting colony keep the young in nurseries called creches once they leave the nests. This behavior provides a measure of protection from marauding gulls who form their own colonies nearby. Awkward on land, the pelican in flight *(facing)* epitomizes grace.
PELECANUS OCCIDENTALIS

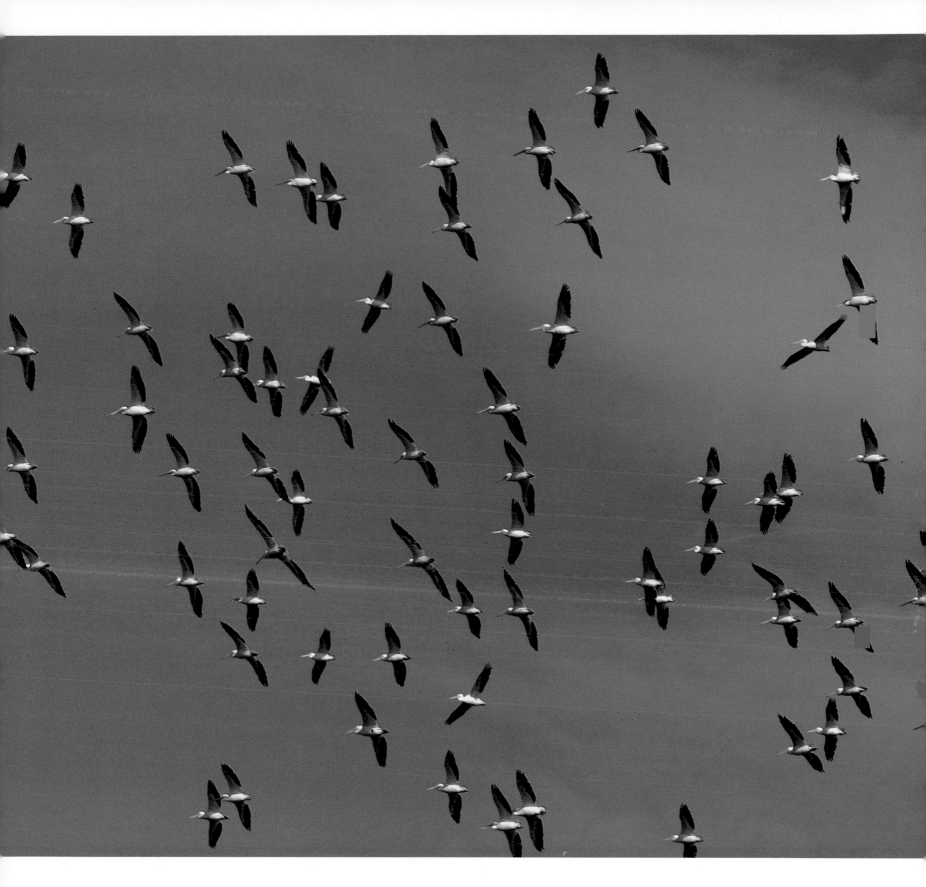

On a sabal palm trunk at Florida's Merritt Island NWR perches a lone wood stork. The stork returns to its breeding grounds at the beginning of the dry season and is dependent on water levels to supply an exact concentration of fish, without which it will not even attempt to nest. Human manipulation of the water table has placed the wood stork on the federal endangered species list.

MYCTERIA AMERICANA

After nesting, wood storks migrate northward to spend summer and early fall in flocks in the lower southeastern United States. The birds in the western part of the mid-South are believed to come from Mexican breeding colonies; those in more eastern states from Florida. Within these summer flocks adults and juveniles can be easily distinguished by beak color: young birds have a yellow beak, adults a browner one.

MYCTERIA AMERICANA

The snowy egret's bright yellow feet contrast with its black legs out of breeding season. It has more feeding strategies than any other heron—several use the yellow feet. The snowy egret sometimes flies low, dragging its feet in the water, then snaps up food that swims to the surface.

EGRETTA THULA

(Facing) For a very brief time at the peak of breeding season the lore, or space between eye and beak, of the great egret takes on a bright green color.

CASMERODIUS ALBUS

Once classified as a separate species called the great white heron, this wading bird is now considered a color phase of the great blue heron. In its slate blue plumage the great blue heron is one of our commonest wading birds. In white plumage it is our rarest, found only in extreme southern Florida.

ARDEA HERODIAS

At sunup on a cold
November morning at Bitter
Lake NWR, New Mexico,
sandhill cranes move out
of their roosting place in
the water to feed in the
fields. A few linger, but
in moments all will desert
the lake.
GRUS CANADENSIS

A limpkin rests along Florida's Wakulla River before foraging for mollusks. The apple snail is a favorite food, although the limpkin is not confined to this diet as is the rarer snail kite. The limpkin's eerie night cries are fabled by locals to be the wails of little boys lost in the trackless swamp.

ARAMUS GUARAUNA

The wind making a regal crown of its
head feathers, a reddish egret pauses
during feeding in a shallow salt lagoon.
Some egrets and herons wait patiently for
food to come to them, but the reddish
egret stands still for only an instant,
jumps wildly to another spot, looks
frantically for prey, then jumps again.
EGRETTA RUFESCENS

A young double-crested cormorant rain-bathes in a Virginia marsh. Cormorants are attracted to all kinds of water—salt, fresh, and brackish.
PHALACROCORAX AURITUS

(Facing) In March an anhinga feeds her nestlings over Taylor Slough in Everglades National Park. The anhinga always catches fish headfirst—it can't swallow a fish tailfirst. The dense population and tameness of these birds have given this delightful spot to observe wildlife the name "Anhinga Trail."
ANHINGA ANHINGA

A male anhinga dries his feathers after fishing. Swimming half-submerged with only neck and head protruding has earned him the popular name "snakebird." His sharp beak is perfectly adapted for fishing. After spearing a fish, he will toss it into the air and catch it with open beak.
ANHINGA ANHINGA